Land of the Peace

Leona Gom

LAND OF THE PEACE © copyright 1980 by Leona Gom

ISBN 0-920066-37-2   (paper)
ISBN 0-920066-38-0   (cloth)

Book design and cover by Neil and Susan Wagner

Published Fall 1980 by

Thistledown Press
668 East Place
Saskatoon, Sask.
S7J 2Z5

Canadian Cataloguing in Publication Data

Gom, Leona, 1946-

    Land of the Peace

        Poems

        ISBN 0-920066-38-0 (bound)
        ISBN 0-920066-37-2 (pbk.)

        I. Title

        PS8563.04L3   C811'54   C81-091002-0

        PR9199.3.G65L3

ACKNOWLEDGEMENTS

Many of the poems in LAND OF THE PEACE have appeared or will appear in the following literary publications:

ARC	MALAHAT REVIEW
ARIEL	MATRIX
CANADIAN FORUM	NEBULA
CVII	NEWEST REVIEW
DALHOUSIE REVIEW	ORIGINS
DANDELION	POETRY CANADA REVIEW
DESCANT	QUARRY
THE FIDDLEHEAD	WAVES
GRAIN	

In addition, some of the poems have appeared or will appear in the following anthologies:

GOING FOR COFFEE (Ed. Tom Wayman)
NEW: WEST COAST (Ed. Fred Candelaria)
END OF THE WORLD SPESHUL (Ed. bill bissett)
ALBERTA DIAMOND JUBILEE ANTHOLOGY (Ed. J. Chalmers)
SIX POETS OF BRITISH COLUMBIA (Ed. Robin Skelton)

Photographs used by permission of Mrs. Mary Gom.
This book has been published with the assistance of the Saskatchewan Arts Board and The Canada Council.

TABLE OF CONTENTS

RECONSTRUCTION

What is left are the chimney bricks, rising
blunt in the fields
like a stack of bones.

They have, from single bones,
reconstructed dinosaurs,
the shape surrounding through history
the remaining fragment
like memory of water clings to drought.
As we watch,
the house shakes itself slowly into place,
log walls climb
around the old bricks,
assemble themselves into roof.
Through the windows
we can see
parallelograms of sunlight
lying on the floor.
Smoke rising from the chimney
is tautology:
we know already there are people inside,
can see their shadows
move across the windows,
hear their lives
        breathing across the whole country.

SETTLERS

the land dreams itself
    its heavy pine forests,
    meadows great with grass
    and grazing deer
the land dreams,
animate into aeons

one day shudders awake,
the pillage of plows
in its back
squeezing an alien seed
like an allergy
prophetic under its skin

NORTH OF TOWN

the fist of this town opens,
cracking its fingers north
across pine and spruce and muskeg

    this is the symbol
        falling on the land
    this is the road
        fitting around itself
        the forest

culverts knuckle under
        its wrinkle-pleated skin;
ditches fall away like dead cells,
        coagulate with old rain

the road points into
the wilderness, to this final
break with metaphor:
        what would fingertip
        becomes tree,
        the road becomes path,
        the path does not leave
        the incomparable forest

TERRY

The children running
                running home
to be the first to tell:
    the tractor rolled over,
    yesterday, yes, after school,
    on the way to the field,
    crushed him, yes.
Eager with disaster,
watching their parents greedily,
knowing that only such news
will make them pause —
        hands for once still
        on the unfinished fences,
        on the axe incomplete over wood —
knowing that only such news
will make them look deeply
            at their children,
see the fields and the farms
make their premature claim,
see their own children
dead under overturned machines.

CHOP

Running the chopper all afternoon,
he was white with dust,
the thick flour of grain.
He would stand in the yard and call,
Staub mich ab, and, reluctant,
I would take the broom and go outside,
and he would turn his back to me,
tensing for the blows.
But I never struck him hard enough,
something in me shy with shame,
the dust scarcely stirring
under my apologetic blows.
Harder, my mother would call,
impatient, from the house,
coming out at last and doing it herself.
Her blows would rock his body,
landing solidly on shoulders, back and legs,
the dust whitening the air;
And me standing back,
a child, inarticulate,
watching the blows fall
and his body absorb them,
in that fine tension
of their understanding,
that easy balance
of their practical love.

DOUBLE STANDARDS (I)

with my father
it was the purple gas incident.
the RCMP appearing
unexpected
in town,
checking our car
and finding purple gas,
and my father protesting
in impeccable shock
he hadn't put it there
— the oldest son, perhaps,
not him —
the officer, impressed
with his indignation,
letting-him-off-this-time.
and later, my father,
laughing,
telling the story,
and I learn
that he lied,
learn for the first time
about duplicity,
about the relativity
of absolutes.

DOUBLE STANDARDS (II)

with my brother
it was the fencer
     the machine
     that sent electric current
     pulsing through
     the barbed wire fences
it doesn't hurt, he said,
laid my trusting hand
between the barbs,
and the shock thrust itself
up my arm.
I jerked my hand away,
looked dumbly at his laughter,
his betrayal.

and sometime later
I held the paw
of my pet dog
against the wire.
it doesn't hurt, I said,
laughing,
laughing.

FARMLAND

     the west end of the field
      was diffcrent.
ragged edges of crops
pleating into riverbank.
and admission of boundaries
beyond the symmetry
of section lines.
the soft collision
of field with space.
the slopes coiling and recoiling
in green parabolas
     folding
        to the final collusion
        with river:
           the conclusion of land
           the beginning

THE STRAP

I was eight
my first day of school
at recess I played like the boys
    mean and tough
delighted with the ease of leadership
my older sister
always held at home

    this will teach you
    how to get along with people
      and the strap burning
    ten times into each palm
    raying along the fingers
    up the arms
    this will teach you
    to play nicely
      and the strap burning
    cutting obedience
    into the open personality
    you might as well learn early
    branding the adult
    into the child

CAPITALISM

The first four years
I rode horseback to school,
    most of the other kids
    coming in by then
    some other way,
    in something motorized
    but less reliable.

So there I was
with the only horse at school,
and it had started to become that time
when horses were a novelty
to my tractor-jaded generation,
and I soon realized
I had a good thing here.

At recess I set up my business:
    a penny a pat
    a nickel a ride
    a dime for the whole noon hour.
There were mishaps, of course,
but generally minor,
    resulting mostly from the horse
    thinking it was home time
    and heading eagerly off,
but this seemed only to add
to the thrill.

Business was good,
and word got around.
Eventually it reached my parents,
and I was ordered to stop,
which even then seemed contrary
to the free-enterprise ethic
I was learning elsewhere, everywhere.
But I was hardly in position
to oppose this government intervention,
so I closed my barn doors,
burned the books,
and that was that.

I confess
to a certain nostalgia
for that carly entrepreneur,
having never since
been so successfully self-employed.

THE TRUE NORTH

we are drawing the maple leaf,
we copy it from a book,
it's our national emblem,
when Laura says,
    *what **is** a maple leaf,*
and we all giggle,
imagine asking that,
why, we all know, it's —
and teacher says,
    why, it's —
    the maple tree leaf,
and Laura says,
    how come
    I never seen one,
and we all gasp,
crayons cringing
over maple leaves,
but teacher looks —
not mad, something else,
she looks —
out the window,
at the thick hair
of poplar and spruce
braided across the sky,
and she says,
    you're right,
    it doesn't grow here,
and we wait,
there must be something more,
but she only says,
    finish your colouring,
and outside
the wind accuses
the unknown forest.

BOX SOCIAL

In elementary school, the teacher decided
        to have a box social,
and all us girls had to bring a box of food,
        wrapped fancy and anonymous,
and then the boys would bid on it
        and win the girl whose box they got.

someone's mom complained,
        it was hard enough
        to feed her own kid,
        not someone else's, too,
        and, besides, her daughter was too young
        for all this stuff.
but the teacher told her patiently
        it was an exercise in role-playing,
        it would prepare us
        to be grown-ups,
and who
could argue
with that?

A CAUTIONARY TALE FOR CHILDREN

She was in the car.
He was two miles down the road.
She was wearing summer shoes and nylons.
He had no mittens.
She was curled in the seat,
          clutching her purse.
He was lying on the side of the road,
          holding a package of matches.

This was our mythology,
our own grim ballad of our history.
We learned it like a prayer.
No foreign fairy-tales,
          witches with their ovens,
          fire-breathing dragons,
          angry sun-gods
          or hell with its eternal flames,
convinced us
fire
was stronger evil
than this cold.

METAMORPHOSIS

something is happening
to this girl.

she stands on one leg
on the third block
of her hopscotch game,
lifts herself forward
to the next double squares,
and, as she jumps,
something changes.

her straight child's body
curls slowly in the air,
the legs that assert themselves
apart on the squares
curve in calf and thigh,
angles become arches;
her arms pumping slowly
to her sides adjust
to a new centre of gravity,
the beginnings of breasts
push at her sweater,
her braids have come undone
and her hair flies loose around her.

behind her
the schoolhouse blurs,
becomes insubstantial
and meaningless,
and the boys in the playground
move toward her,
something sure and sinister
in their languid circling.

slowly she picks up the beanbag.
when she straightens,
her face gathers
the bewildered awareness
of the body's betrayal,
the unfamiliar feel
of the child's toy
in her woman's hand.

PEN-PALS

We wrote with all
the ardour of discovery,
boxes of letters
chronicling our adolescence,
fluent confessions
leaping back and forth
in the merciful mail.

And then our meeting.
He asked if I got his last letter.
Yes, I said,
and the conversation
crumbled from there,
both of us sensing with panic
our mistake,
thinking how we later might
discuss it as abstraction
in premeditated prose,
but knowing already
that everything was changed,
that our letters would fold up
into them now
a great emptiness,
a failure
we could never articulate.

It was left, then, just
to make the graceful end:
the reserved notes,
sent further and further apart
until there were none at all,
only the boxes of old letters

we threw away,
like our childhood,
with longing
and relief.

THE CITY AT THE END OF IT

a slow collage of expectation
assuming the white canvas
of my adolescence,
the city at last
lifted before me
like the sun on a dark horizon,
moving past the bus windows
all glow and promise;
my face in the glass superimposed,
city and self
the same portrait

so far before I would see
the painting finished and flawed,
and the city crumpled
like an oily rag
on the rim of the landscape.

BLIZZARDS

it was
    he said
the horizontal snow
that drove her mad
    blowing in thin and endless chains
    across our windows

not pulling itself down
into the reason of the right angle
    but that constant tearing across
eroding the expectation of gravity
       the vertical reassurance
       on the flat landscape

there was only
that white streaming
into the corners of her eyes
across the pointless prairie

THAT OLD WAR

at first
when the sun triumphed daily in the sky,
she stood angry in her burning
fields, heads of wheat
          crumbling in her hands,
her eyes that followed
any tatters of cloud
waiting for a rebellious puff
of cumulus

but as day after day
she walked through her defeat
the sun conquered even her anger,
and she yielded like her crops
to the slow famine
of next year
    next year

JAPANESE ORANGES

there was Christmas
in the box with them
and their perfect sections
bursting between our teeth
was like unwrapping presents
but there was other pleasure
in the purchase
      the wooden box to use again
      the squares of orange tissue
      that would relieve
      the brittle newspapers
      and catalogues
      as toilet paper

it was a time of no waste
of satisfaction
in complete consumption

MOTHER WITH CHILD

She rocks the jar of cream
in her lap
like a cranky child,
tries to lull it
to some expected form,
as I see myself
rocked so often
on that tired lap.
Finally, late at night,
the cream thickens, clots,
she pours off the buttermilk,
gives me a glass.
Thank God that's done, she says,
and goes to bed.
I watch the pale hill of butter,
wonder if my own
murky childhood's end
met with such relief,
a sudden falling together
into one shape,
no more weary rocking, rocking
late into the night.

MY MOTHER / MY SELF

loving the sharp gassy smell
of the new mantles,
I would lean close
as my father pumped up
    and lit the lamp,
and suddenly my hair was on fire,
    a wild corona of flame
    around my head,
and my mother from across the kitchen
instantly there,
beating the flames out
with her hands.

it has become
part of the apocrypha
I carry with me
from age to age,
    that story,
seeming with the years
more allegory than truth,
but leaving me always
the guilty daughter
    safe
in the scarred hands
of her mother.

FOUR WE KNEW

This one hemorrhaged to death
by chopping wood
until her tenth child broke
vengefully from body.

This one, whose husband died,
had a son of nine who,
knowing he was now the man
and to assume his father's place,
stabbed her when she disobeyed.

This one took her life inside herself
and existed empty for a year,
until her body understood
and hanged itself in the barn.

This one was beaten
every Sunday after church,
for the sins of Eve, her husband said,
it says in the Bible

    In rehearsal,
    on Saturdays, four girls, fourteen,
    in Confirmation Class,
    reciting our end of childhood;
    taught what it would mean
    to be women in the Church:
    men obey God,
    and women their husbands.

PUNISHMENTS

I remember most
being locked in the dark cellar,
the musty earth sealing around me,
the rustle of unseen creatures
in the monstrous corners,
my throat and fingers raw
from imploring the deaf door.
When we were older
the discipline was more direct,
always our images of him
the raised hand,
the freshly-cut switch,
the brutal belt.
That we learned to love him
is not, they tell us, surprising.
That we learned to understand
and to forgive
the tortured child in him
perhaps is.

THE LAST PICTURE OF MY FATHER

In the last picture of my father
he is sitting in his old chair,
his fingers white and unused on his lap,
the smile on his papery face
having nothing to do
with the cancer
scribbling its ugly address
across his skin,
or with the desperate talismans
we piled around him:
      on his left,
      the garish Christmas tree,
      presents effusive under it,
      on his right,
      myself, his daughter,
      young and wearing make-up
      and a green dress.
It is only, I have pointed out,
the colour film
that makes our eyes red,
we were all so careful
not to cry.

CANCER

The curtain pulling suddenly
        across the open window,
a blotter sucking up
        the white ink of the sun;
it stains a pale circle
        on the cloth.
And we, for the first time
in this darkening room,
can stare unblinded at the light
and see your death interposed.

DUSK

a dark wing
   slitting
the pale belly of sky,
the hawk
   slides
into the west.
a small death
hangs in its claws.

a dangerous evening.

later,
the bone-white moon
litters the landscape.

THE LAST

your death
   like a sealed envelope
and all my words to you
   unsent

RAW MATERIAL

One day contained it:
my mother in the morning
chasing for miles across the fields
a hawk with a chicken
heavy in its talons,
her slapping at it with a broom
until she knocked the chicken
down and safe.
and in the afternoon my brother,
rifle over his young male shoulder,
carrying home by the ears
the damp brown body
of a rabbit.

A day so rich in implications:
I wait for the connection,
the pulse across the synapse,
but the images seal shut like seeds,
fact impervious to symbol.

NAZIS

Nazis, the whispers began,
Nazis, when they gathered
and poured over each other
memory of the Old Country
to wash away the dust
of the cold Canadian fields.
Nazis, the voices said
to their backs in the town,
Nazis, to their children
bewildered at school,
Nazis, until they kept alien
to their farms and afraid.

Such relief for us all,
the end of the war,
the enemy now redefined,
the stooped Ukrainians
pausing over their plows,
Communists, we said.
Communists.

IMMIGRANTS

"If Canada is to remain a white man's country,
it can ill afford to be the dumping ground for
the scum of Europe." Saturday Night, 1921

English like a stone in their mouths,
they translated their lives
into the rhetoric of this country,
plowing the old languages
into the deaf soil,
the anglican rhythms of the factories.

And it comes to this:
their children Canadian
and foreigners to them,
their children, proudly unilingual,
ashamed of the outgrown dialects,
and of the fluent labour
of their parents' lives.

THE WAY HE TOLD IT

Such cold,
the horses white with it,
and my wife, dying,
in the sleigh,
forty miles to hospital,
then getting there,
and they wouldn't take her in.
No money, no doctor,
they said.
And Rosenbloom, he was there,
you take this woman in, he yelled,
I'll pay your goddamned money!
So then it was all right,
they would take her in.
He was a Jew, Rosenbloom, they said,
but this is what I remember of him.

COLLUSION

It is the dog in everyone's past,
the one that dies,
the one that returns in the night
with its usher of flies,
its face bloody and blind,
nuzzling our sleep,
the one that always finds the child
connecting for the first time
the rifle shot
with the absent animal,
connecting forever
the knowledge
with the guilt.

A LOT TO KILL

There was always a lot to kill,
the being, reason enough.
Bears springing reborn from the earth,
hawks multiplying even in the rifle shot,
lynx and deer regenerating in the dim forest,
the forest itself darkening forever
            beyond the eye of the axe.
The wilderness limitless,
our killing of it then,
the last without guilt.

ENERGY

One of the jobs
was putting up ice in winter,
cutting the big blocks from the dugout,
hauling them to the icehouse.
And then, that miraculous discovery
in burning July,
of the cold still crystallized
in the sawdust,
and me asking my father
why we couldn't save
pieces of heat from summer
the same way.
Him waving at the woodpile
he was building,
saying, there it is,
and it was one of those
epiphanies of childhood,
one of life's great harmonies understood,
and our place in it.

THE FARMERS' UNION

It was poverty
forced the first co-operation,
      the threshing crews
      the wood-cutting teams
      the machines jointly-owned,
pushed them,
    overalled immigrants
    educated by injustice,
    to the picket lines in '47,
and led the co-op movement,
      the twine that bound them together
      simple and profound
      as bundles of grain.

They shake their heads
about their children.
Having enough to eat
makes them careless, they say.
Around them
the family farms
become hungry corporations,
elevators marked Co-op
become Cargill,
no one bothers with binders any more,
or threshing crews,
or binder twine.

COW

Sometime becomes a precedent,
a referent.
For example.
The child, milking the cow.
The child has learned
the slow, stroking preliminaries,
the bonding of milker and cow
before she lets down her milk.
The child pulls it into the pail
in an easy, tinny rhythm.
        — the cats in a careful semi-circle
        gulping greedy at the stream
        that shatters in their faces —
The pail fills,
settles heavy on the heels of the child,
head against the warm flank,
almost asleep
        — the smell of the frothy milk,
                    the cow,
                    the hay-hung barn —

And some infant philosophy drifts past,
something about being happy,
about doing a job quietly and well —
        And then:
suddenly, the rear foot has lifted, kicked,
    the milk stool topples
    the child clutches at pail
               at cow
               at air
    everything is flying
    milk-covered cats are streaking away —
And the child is sitting
in a pool of muck and milk,
staring at the cow
with her foot in the pail.

    This is the precedent,
the sequence indelible.
And the adult wary
at every complacency,
remembering the cow
with her foot in the pail.

PIG

They say you make a good pet
    (I have seen you taken for walks
    on a leash in a Major American City
    with a red bow around your neck)
They say you are more intelligent than dogs
    (Yes — dogs have the I.Q. of Q-tips)
They say you are a good watchpig
    (I imagine you crouching wary
    at night in my living room
    baring your teeth)
They say beauty is in a pig's eye

There is no doubt
your image has changed

Someday I will sit in my senile city chair
and tell stories to your descendants
sitting on their bored haunches at my feet
    of the barbaric days
when you were bred for food
like the first Pekinese
    of unjust epithets
like "wallowing" and "filthy"
ascribed to you
    of you anarchic through fences
plundering gardens
and galloping gracelessly down country roads
with us in furious pursuit
    of all those unenlightened days
when we were simply farmers
and you were simply swine

STONE

There is something in stones
that blisters them annually up
from the earth
against the logic of gravity,
that grows them like calluses
on the palms of spring fields.

Like the first sea creatures
compelled to the blue air, the sun,
they squeeze themselves to the surface,
shoulder their way
through the passive soil,
and hold their grey and enigmatic faces
to the light:
an assertion of rock,
fragments of an old message
we will collect and haul away.

LANDSCAPE

it has become
the Abandoned Farmhouse Genre.
in the upper right
is always the grey house
decaying into the ground
and surrounded
by much artistic space.
sometimes a rusting plow
appears to the left of the house,
and a few rotted fence posts
lean listlessly in the foreground.
there are seldom trees,
and they never have leaves.
the colours are always dark, dull,
but the rigid line of the horizon
must somewhere bisect the scene.

yet,
in even the most sentimental of these,
if we look closely,
closely,
we can see the dead farm is real,
a vestigial memory
softening behind the brittle paint,
a real loss,
an unmanipulated sorrow.

FARM WOMEN

to Irene Murdoch

you labour for years
in the cold fields of this country,
in the hot kitchens of your houses,
in the birthing of unwanted children

    (you do what you must
    there is
    no other choice you
    survive)

to this final appraisal
in a man's court of law:
your easeless years
rewarded with a feudal wage,
   your room and board;
your work betrayed as
     just a normal contribution for a wife

and you sit
with your large-knuckled hands
crumpled on your laps,
beyond even anger
as you see the empty harvests of your lives,
your plantings doomed from the start
by the dry injustice
of these judgements:
     your work worthless,
     the farms theirs

ELEGY

for S.

It is necessary, she said,
to write about the workers,
the factory labourers and farmers,
the immigrants, the poor,
it is necessary, she said
(stroking the confessional poems
trivialized in our laps),
to make their laboured lives
our literature,
all else is solipsism, she said,
goading her young self
into those old sorrows.

To speak
for her surrendered life
is also
necessary.

PICTURE OF THE WIDOW

In this photograph
she stands as she stood
for three weeks after,
silent on the shore,
the boneless fingers
of the river
plaiting his death
into her eyes.

     watching
     for some sign,
     something to surface
     an oar to wash ashore,
     anything.

     perhaps trying to learn
     that efficient energy
     of indifference.

     or the other,
     the answer accessible
     in her own obedient body,
     feeling already
     the cold astonishing her feet,
     the pull of current
     at her thighs
     like a reunion,
     everything abstracted
     resuming perspective,
     a final focussing in
     before the shutter
     blinks shut.

WILD BERRIES

the wild berries on the riverbank
      that swell in the pagan sun
      seduced by a tawny season
      sucking blossoms to berries
      and berries to burning
ripen careless
on this arm of earth

raspberries darken
to no purpose but the sun's
slide slowly from their cores
      drop
among the leaves
like unused words

blueberries
strawberries
tug anarchic from the soil
    stipple the grass
globe into anagrams
    coded messages
    keyed to perception

saskatoons sleeving their branches
    in wet clusters
contain also the dead raisin
        the completed stone
are yet at this moment
accessible as a syllogism
    as the hand reaching

MOSQUITOES

When the winter liquifies at last,
runs wet fingers
through the roots of fields
leaks into dams and dugouts and sloughs
tadpoles already darken the water
like an armada.
There is little time for truce
between the adamant seasons,
before the summer sags with insects,
our skins tear like gauze
beneath their procreative purpose.
The heavy air coagulates
with their survival.

SCHOOLS

It is an understandable indulgence
(you have all done this),
a conscious wading in nostalgia.
    You stand outside the old school,
you let the memories tide over you,
you walk up the stairs, down the hallway,
you let the memories tide over you,
you stop outside the last classroom.
    Look in (the memories tide over you),
it is all still the same,
time has scarcely rippled this place,
the students, you almost remember the faces,
the same desks (the memories),
the teacher is the same,
the lesson the same (tide over you).
    You want to rush in,
to tell them . . .
something important,
to give them answers
the teacher has no questions for,
to shout, *this is what life is, this!*
    You do not, of course, go in,
and they bend their familiar,
their strangers', heads to work,
and you walk away.
    What have you learned, after all,
that they would need to know?

HORSEPOWER

Once,
   horses knew poverty.
Once,
   horses bowed their heads shamefully
   into their collars,
   grateful for the blinders
   that hid their eyes
   from the pompous pity
   of neighbours
   with new tractors.
Once,
   horses were humilated
   by the swaggering machines.

But the horse has made a comeback!
There is a revival of the horse!
Horses have right-of-way at intersections!
Horses can intimidate imported cars
and stare down two-ton trucks.
Horses have become sophisticated;
they trot haughtily around suburban paddocks
and are obligatory ornaments for acreages.
Horses know that every hobby farmer needs them
or would be sneered back to the inner city.
Horses have found a new sense of worth;
a horse is everyone's idea of success.

Is it any wonder
   horses are becoming snobs?
Can you blame them
   for being embarrassed
   at their working-class origins?
Wouldn't *you* try to cover up
   that bastard country Clydesdale
   in your family tree?
Horses have as much right to be bourgeois as we do;
their parents worked hard to give them a good life.
Remember that
   the next time
   one bullies you off the road
   on your way to work
   on his way home
   from a party.

CAT AND MOUSE

He lies before it
like a voluptuary,
licking his fur.
    The mouse moves,
he is on it,
shakes it in his mouth,
bats it with his paw,
but will not kill it,
lets it loose and terrified
to cower in its corner.
    I know that I should kill
the mouse in mercy,
even raise the billet above it
like an absolution
        remember the hayfields
        of childhood
        the last mound lifted
        and my pitchfork
        clattering down
        on the scattering mice
        without this adult fear
        of creating death
    I cannot.
    I lower the billet in shame,
wonder which of us
most civilized.

CIVILIZATION

It is not easy
to come to terms with eating meat.
There are those
who have become vegetarians,
    an impeccable choice.
But there are others
who have become hunters,
    stalking from their suburban homes
    and accepting, they say,
    the implications of their hunger,
    restoring the connection
    between necessity and action.
    (It is never, of course,
    because they like killing.)
I admit,
wary of the primal logic of their argument,
that on the farm we hunted and butchered,
    all the headless carcasses
    strung up outside the barn,
    draining into the red earth,
but it was a necessary chore,
no more than that,
abandoned with relief
for the cellophane-wrapped packages in stores —
    the consequence of income,
    of simple division of labour.
What purist could wish that away?

ARROWHEADS

For years we collected arrowheads,
the flints like dark tongues
mute under our plows and shovels.
Incomplete legends
clenched into centuries of silence,
they persist
in this forgetful land
      (homestead land:
        we are the owners,
        we are the settlers,
        we are the first).
They persist,
and us only inheritors
of a people
that buried its blood
under our thick crops.

      At the muscum, at last,
      they kept only a few.
      A dime a dozen, they said
The memories so cheap, eventually,
and all of us harvesting
still that history.

PIECES

I keep dreaming of Renate
    my first friend
with whom I stumbled
through grades one and two and on
    attached by the forbidden language
    we whispered to each other
through junior high and high school
    as intense in our avowals
    as any sexual lovers
then the drifting apart
and now the dreams
    incomplete
    urging some summation

I found where she lived
I wrote
she answered
    a housewife
    with children
    no shadow on the page
    of the years erased
    of the girl she had been
        I had been
and what did I expect?

there are still the dreams
    dragging their pieces
    of lost personalities
    into my sleep
but they are less frequent
and   like our lives
more closed

REMEMBERING IT

the facts:
    that I was driving home
      through the reserve
      and there were three of them
      on the roadside
    that one was carrying
      a bottle by the neck
      like a dead bird
      and threw it
      at a rock on the road
    that the other two, laughing,
      grabbed him
      and threw him
      in front of my car
    that I swerved,
      the car sheered into the ditch,
      the soft thud of hitting him,
      and then that clean accidental silence.

and how it changed:

   i.   he stumbles from under my bumper,
       staggers down the road with his friends
       past the bottle become shards on the road

   ii.   *you stupid bastards,* I shout,
       watching them go.
       I could have been killed, I think,
       they could have damned well killed me

   iii.   when they have gone,
       three fenceposts leaning across a field,
       I get out of the car,
       examine the fender for damage

HARVEST

I listen to the pioneers
in their tiny retirement houses in town,
rooms thick
with old furniture and photographs.
One shelf or bureau blooms
with pictures of distant grandchildren,
but there is little else of the present here;
even the clocks chiming the hour
sound years behind.

They show me their albums,
ripe with harvests
      themselves young
        in fields of chest-high wheat,
      the threshing crews,
      new barns and new children
        inheriting the land behind them
        still full with forest.

They tell me of the good-old-days,
and then they laugh,
waving at the walls folding them in,
and say,
      we never had it so good,
      running water and electricity,
      such miracles!
and of course it is true,
of course
it is true.

ALBERTA

The country broods about Alberta.
    Alberta no longer knows its place,
    Alberta is boom-town,
    Alberta is suddenly rich.
Edmonton and Calgary gloat
on their skylines,
prosperity fattening overnight
the lean new office buildings.

The north has no new affluence.
The old towns still stumble
    along the roadsides,
their roads still crumble
    into washboard gravel, into dirt.
Among the trees
homesteads sink empty into the earth.
Farmers stand
like archetypes
in their tired fields.

The moneyed murmurs of the southern cities
drift past like rumours of rain.

ELEVATORS

These Quebec villages
gather the countryside
into huge spires,
extorting benediction from the skies.
Houses kneel like supplicants
at their feet.

The churches in the prairie towns
are much more modest,
indistinguishable on the horizon.
The true temples here,
garnering the countryside,
declare themselves more quickly to the eye.
Huge eruptions on the backs of the towns,
they petition the skies
with their blunt heads
and their homages of grain.

NEW SOIL

A letter from my mother,
she wonders again
about selling the farm.
You, repotting the ivy.
Jesus, you say *look at this,*
and I see the roots have grown
into the sides of the pot,
and you have had to slice them off
to free the plant.
It lies dishevelled in its old dirt
as we prepare
a new pot, new soil.

MEN, SNORING

He could awe us all, my father,
with his barbarous snores,
that warfare in his throat
that fired his breath
in staccato volleys
across the room at us,
plundering our evenings.
How do you sleep? I asked my mother,
who could wake to a whisper.
I don't hear it, she said,
which I did not believe,
and filed in memory
under Mother's Martyrdom.

My own men,
when it came my time,
I chose from their sleep,
the Silent Slumberers,
breath easing gently from them
as they lay curled on their sides;
some, I did allow
a placid dream
to bubble from their open mouths,
and later I would even tolerate
those purring gently in their sleep
like cats.

But this one, the last one —
he saws the proverbial logs
of his sleep
with a chainsaw;
his snores have loosened
plaster on the ceiling,
have homogenized the left-overs
in the refrigerator,
have shattered light bulbs
and frightened plants to death.
How do you sleep? asks my mother.
Quite well, I reply.

REUNION

Shopping in the IGA,
she looked like the mother
of the girl I knew,
her familiar features
squeezed into the fleshy face,
the dark hair, defeated with grey,
pulling up from her forehead
in that same startled wave.
You haven't changed, I say,
succumbing stupidly to ritual.
She tells me of her children,
     three furtive mad-eyed creatures
     dropped in the aisles around her
     like bruised vegetables,
of the failed farm,
the small-town disgrace of welfare.
I tell her of the city.
When at last we lapse awkwardly apart,
some obligatory time
for such meetings having passed,
she says suddenly,
don't pity me, you know,
and I only stare at her,
my guilt so manifest
it has no defense,
and we turn away,
into the unimagined lives
neither of us has chosen,
so much to pity in both of us.

THESE POEMS

these poems are homesick
they keep crawling out
        from under my pen
and running back
        to the north
they will not be domesticated
they will not be toilet-trained
they mess all over the page
with their persistent images
        of farm
they chew through their ropes
        of urban metaphors
and sneak away whenever they can
and when there is no way out
they curl up spitefully
        underneath their titles
and starve themselves
        to death

WEST

(In the late 1960s, over 100 Toronto residents set out in a covered-wagon caravan for the Peace River country in Alberta, where they had heard homestead land was still available. The expedition barely made it out of Ontario before the last of its families dropped out due to financial ruin or disillusionment.)

We failed, yes.
Our friends smile
behind their guise of sympathy.
They knew we'd never make it.
They fold us back
into our thin apartment buildings,
our jobs at the ends of hallways.

We failed, yes.
Our friends smile.
We were anachronisms,
they say,
inheriting a pastoral need
a century too late.
We cannot argue.
They are right.
You'd just have turned it
into city, they insist.
Perhaps, we say,
looking across the taut streets
strung like barbed wire
below us.

But daily the dream
pulls itself across our lives,
soft and unexpected
as cobwebs on our faces.
It nudges our sleep
into the open land,
the acres lying like a revelation
before us,
green and unpeopled.

LAND OF THE PEACE

Unrolling out of the mountains
at Chetwynd,
the land reveals itself
like an alphabet,
the characters thrusting up yellow
in chapters of rapeseed and wheat.

I pronounce the names of this place
carefully,
waiting for the dialect
to assert itself
over the language
of city and mountain and ocean.
But the syllables resist,
the words do not remember me;
my voice is the sound
of the stranger.

MECHANICS

it is the car's perceptions now
that label the journey.
    the hardtop at last grates into gravel,
      the dust clouds opaquing the road,
    gravel foams into dirt,
    dirt becomes two rutted tracks,
    the declarative grass
      lisps between the wheels.

and the house at the end of it,
    framed in the spattered windshield
    like a smudged painting,
leans into the ground,
heavy with its emptiness.

I wait for whatever it is
I came here for
to find me,
but the car idles uneasily under me.
I am too far in my future
to remember alternatives,
    the bare feet
    in the warm dirt;
the car threatening to stall
chooses my direction.
I back up,
  turn around.

the tires wind up the thread of my coming,
pushing quickly through the mazes of dust
to the smooth clairvoyance of pavement.

SOUTH

driving south from childhood,
remembrance banked at the roadsides
          like snow,
blowing in threads
          across my vision;
it tries to sew shut the road,
          but the wipers run
          their skeletal fingers
          through the easy weave;
everything is memory and white,
I move in white stasis
     south
          south
              (the snow dampens)
                   south
                      (melts)
south to another season
          twenty years away;
the grass at the sides of these roads
has never been young.

GEOLOGICAL TIME

When you enter this house
you become an archaeologist,
cautiously peeling away strata
of wallpaper, linoleum, paint, wood,
each new, old pattern
throbbing into years of memories,
more and more clouded
until you are not sure
if you have passed beyond
your own birth in this place,
to inherited knowledge,
some collective unconscious
lathered like mortar
between the final logs.

You find the artifacts,
predictable derelicts of evolution,
the cracked washbasin, the rusted flatiron,
the brittle calendar with elliptical memos:
May 10: fescue, November 24: Eaton's order.
Pencil lines climb
up a mottled doorframe,
was it you who stood there,
and who measured your growth,
marks like hieroglyphics
you almost understand?

You need the beginnings,
the first excavation,
the root cellar
down the crumbling steps,
into the primal dark,
a few jars of preserves
far back on the earth shelves,
vegetables like soft fossils
ambiguous in their bins,
nothing you can use,
nothing in all these pieces
that defines you
beyond a random genesis
ricocheting across history,
nothing to tell you finally
where you are from,
why you changed,
what you have become.

Leona Gom was born and grew up in the Peace River country of northern Alberta. She now lives on the west coast and teaches at Douglas College. Her first book of poems, KINDLING (Fiddlehead Poetry Books) appeared in 1972 and her second, SINGLETREE (Sono Nis Press) was published in 1975. Leona Gom's poems have appeared in publications across North America and in Australia. She has also appeared in at least ten poetry anthologies.

THISTLEDOWN BOOKS

WIND SONGS by Glen Sorestad
DARK HONEY by Ronald Marken
INSIDE IS THE SKY by Lorna Uher
OCTOMI by Andrew Suknaski
SUMMER'S BRIGHT BLOOD by William Latta
PRAIRIE PUB POEMS by Glen Sorestad
PORTRAITS by Lala Koehn
HAIL STORM by Peter Christensen
BETWEEN THE LINES by Stephen Scriver
GATHERING FIRE by Helen Hawley
TOWARDS A NEW COMPASS by Lorne Daniel
NOW IS A FAR COUNTRY by John V. Hicks
OLF WIVES LAKE by J.D. Fry
THE CURRIED CHICKEN APOCALYPSE by Michael Cullen
ANCESTRAL DANCES by Glen Sorestad
EAST OF MYLOONA by Andrew Suknaski
BLUE SUNRISE by Bert Almon
THE MUSHROOM JAR by Nancy Senior
WINTER YOUR SLEEP by John V. Hicks
DIRT HILLS MIRAGE by Barbara Sapergia
LAND OF THE PEACE by Leona Gom